Chris Bosh

THE STORY OF THE MIAMI HEAT

Tyler Herro

A HISTORY OF HOOPS

THE STORY OF THE

MIAMI
HEAT

JIM WHITING

Dion Waiters

CREATIVE EDUCATION / CREATIVE PAPERBACKS

Published by Creative Education and Creative Paperbacks
P.O. Box 227, Mankato, Minnesota 56002
Creative Education and Creative Paperbacks are imprints of
The Creative Company
www.thecreativecompany.us

Design and production by Blue Design (www.bluedes.com)
Art direction by Rita Marshall

Photographs by Corbis (Victor Baldizon, Hans Deryk), Getty (Isaac Baldizon, Victor Baldizon, Andrew D. Bernstein, Nathaniel S. Butler, Lou Capozzola, Angelo Cavalli, Mike Ehrmann, Jesse D. Garrabrant, John Iacono, Mitchell Lef, Peter Llewellyn, Andy Lyons, John W. McDonough, Jim McIsaac, Fernando Medina, Manny Millan, Greg Nels on, Michael Reaves, Bob Rosato, Jamie Squire), © Steve Lipofsky, Newscom (Frederic J. Brown, Robert Duyos, Ting Shen/Xinhua/Photoshot), USPresswire (David Butler II)

Library of Congress Cataloging-in-Publication Data
Names: Whiting, Jim, 1943- author.
Title: The story of the Miami Heat / By Jim Whiting.
Description: Mankato, Minnesota : Creative Education and Creative
  Paperbacks, [2023] | Series: Creative Sports: A History of Hoops |
  Includes index. | Audience: Ages 8-12 |
  Audience: Grades 4-6 | Summary: "Middle grade basketball fans are
  introduced to the extraordinary history of NBA's Miami Heat with a
  photo-laden narrative of their greatest successes and losses"-- Provided
  by publisher.
Identifiers: LCCN 2022016891 (print) | LCCN 2022016892 (ebook) | ISBN
  9781640266322 (library binding) | ISBN 9781682771884 (paperback) | ISBN
  9781640007734 (pdf)
Subjects: LCSH: Miami Heat (Basketball team)--History--Juvenile literature.
  | Miami Heat (Basketball team)--Biography--Juvenile literature.
Classification: LCC GV885.52.M53 W455 2023 (print) | LCC GV885.52.M53
  (ebook) | DDC 796.323/6409759381--dc23
LC record available at https://lccn.loc.gov/2022016891
LC ebook record available at https://lccn.loc.gov/2022016892

LeBron James

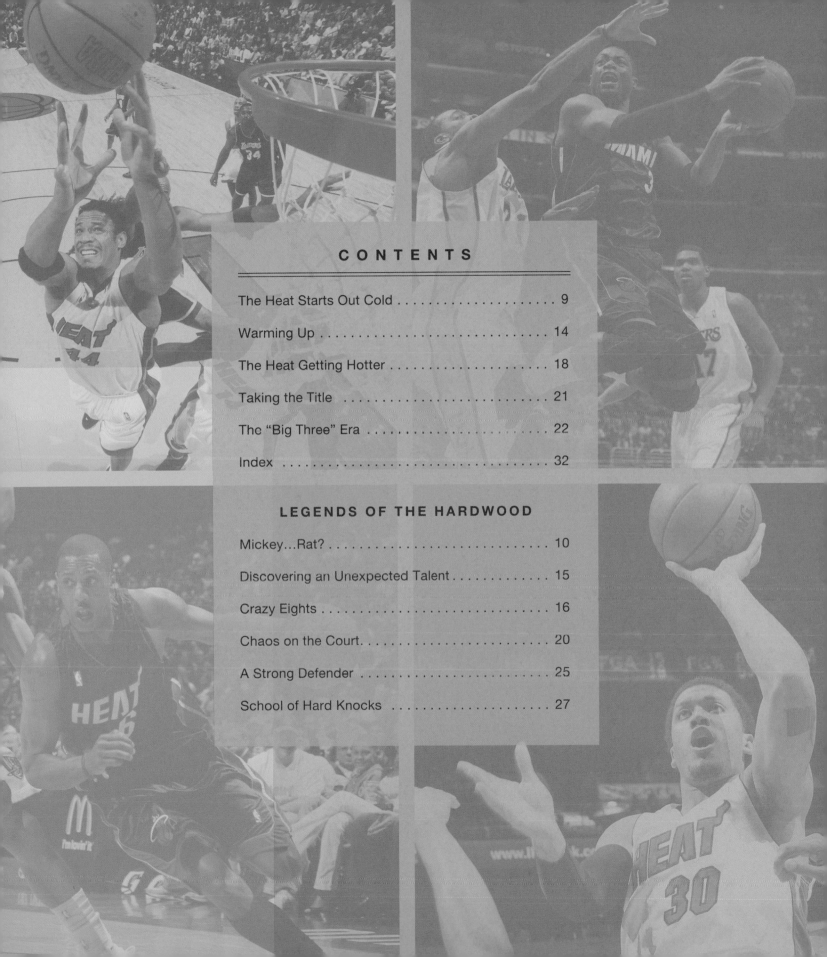

CONTENTS

LEGENDS OF THE HARDWOOD

THE HEAT STARTS OUT COLD

The Miami Heat seemed destined to lose the 2013 NBA (National Basketball Association) Finals. The San Antonio Spurs led Game 6 by 5 points with just 28 seconds left. They were already up 3 games to 2 over the Miami Heat. League officials acted like the game was over. They surrounded the court with bright yellow tape to keep spectators off.

Heat small forward LeBron James sank a three-point shot eight seconds later. San Antonio scored a free throw moments later to go up by three points. The Heat worked the ball around, looking for an open shot. It came to James with eight seconds remaining. He missed a game-tying three-point shot. Miami power forward Chris Bosh had just entered the game to provide extra height. The move

MIAMI HEAT

9

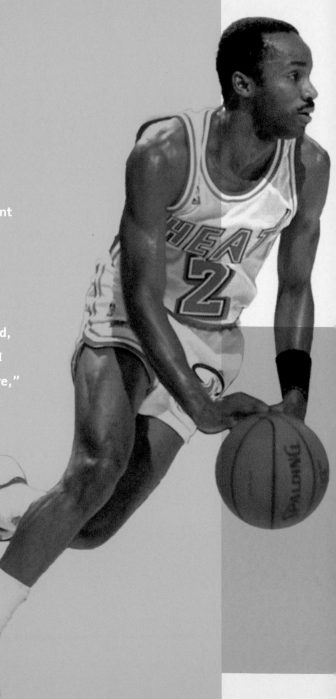

Rory Sparrow in 1989

MICKEY...RAT?

For many years, Miami was Florida's most important city. But in 1971, Disney World opened in Orlando. Other theme parks soon followed. The two cities competed for tourist dollars. The situation grew worse when they competed for an NBA franchise. Patrick Williams, a representative for Orlando's bid, pointed out Miami's reputation for crime. "When I approached the checkout counter of a Miami store," he joked, "the salesclerk said, 'Cash, charge, or stickup?'" Miami fought back. "We don't have Mickey Mouse here," said city manager Cesar Odio, "but then, we're not a Mickey Mouse city, either." The ultimate insult came when a Miami newspaper called Mickey Mouse a rat. Awarding franchises to both cities helped end that battle.

paid off. He soared above two Spurs players to snatch the rebound. He fired the ball to shooting guard Ray Allen, who was alone just beyond the three-point line in the right corner. He drained the shot with 5.2 seconds left to send the game into overtime.

James's short jumper at the 1:43 mark in overtime gave Miami a 101–100 lead. The Spurs had possession with just a few seconds left and looked to take the lead. Then Allen stole the ball. He was immediately fouled. He sank two free throws as the Heat won 103–100. "It was by far the best game that I've ever been a part of," James said.

The series wasn't over. In Game 7, Miami led by just two points with 30 seconds remaining. Then James scored four points and shooting guard Dwyane Wade added a free throw as Miami won 95–88 to secure the championship. It was their third championship in eight seasons.

This success was a far cry from the team's origin nearly 30 years earlier. In the mid-1980s, the NBA was rapidly increasing in popularity. Several cities without teams wanted in on the action. Early in 1987, the NBA's expansion committee

recommended adding Minnesota and Charlotte, North Carolina. They also suggested adding a team in Florida. Both Miami and Orlando wanted that franchise. The two cities had long been commercial rivals. Now they launched media attacks on each other. The NBA moved quickly to defuse the problem. It said *both* cities would get teams. Miami would begin play in the 1988–89 season, with Orlando joining the following year. Officials of the new Miami team asked fans for name ideas. Thousands responded. Barracudas, Beaches, and Flamingos were just a few. Several suggested Heat. "The Heat was it," said team official Zev Buffman. "When you think of Miami, that's what you think of."

When fans thought of Miami in the first season, they thought of losses. Lots of losses. The team set an NBA record by losing its first 17 games. The Heat finally notched its first win on December 14. They defeated the Los Angeles Clippers, 89–88. The Heat finished the season 15–67. It was the worst record in the NBA. Rookie Rony Seikaly was a bright spot. He established himself as one of the league's best centers.

The Heat chose sharpshooting small forward Glen Rice in the 1989 NBA Draft. His University of Michigan team had won the 1989 NCAA title. He set a still-standing record of 184 points in a single tournament. But the team continued to struggle. Miami won just 18 games in 1989–90 and 24 the following season. Better days lay ahead. "The Heat have put together a nice group of kids," said Los Angeles Lakers coach Pat Riley. "If they give them some time to grow up, they'll have a good team."

Glen Rice

WARMING UP

iami improved to 38–44 in 1991–92. The Heat qualified for the playoffs for the first time. But the defending champion Chicago Bulls swept the series. After the Heat failed to make the playoffs the following season, Rice challenged his teammates. "We're not kids anymore," he said. "The fans have been patient with us. Now it's time to reward them."

The Heat listened to Rice. They finished 42–40 in 1993–94. It was the team's first winning record. Miami faced the top-seeded Atlanta Hawks in the playoffs. The Heat took a 2–1 series lead before Atlanta rallied to win the next two games. The Heat couldn't maintain the momentum the following season. They dropped to 32 wins.

Team officials made a key move before the 1995–96 season. They hired Pat Riley as coach. He already had four NBA titles to his credit. "We're going to build this franchise into a winner the only way I know how," he said. "We're going to bring in the best players, and we'll work harder than anyone else." He reshaped the roster, bringing in players such as All-Star center Alonzo Mourning and lightning-quick point guard Tim Hardaway. Miami won 42 games and faced Chicago in the playoffs. The Bulls had won an NBA record 72 games. Chicago swept the best-of-five series, winning each of the three games by an average of 23 points.

Riley continued to tinker with the roster. The result was a surprising 61–21 season in 1996–97. Miami won the Atlantic Division of the NBA's Eastern

RONY SEIKALY
CENTER
HEIGHT: 6-FOOT-11
HEAT SEASONS: 1988–94

DISCOVERING AN UNEXPECTED TALENT

Born in Lebanon, Rony Seikaly played high school hoops in Athens, Greece. In those pre-internet days, no one in the U.S. had ever heard of him. During a visit to his brother, who was attending Colgate University, Seikaly dropped by a summer basketball camp run by Syracuse University coach Jim Boeheim. Boeheim was impressed with his size and invited him to play pickup games against current and former Syracuse players. Boeheim recognized Seikaly's raw talent and offered him a scholarship. He became a second-team All-American in his senior year with Syracuse. The school retired his number. He was the Heat's first-ever draft choice and ranks among the top 10 in several all-time Miami career records.

MIAMI HEAT

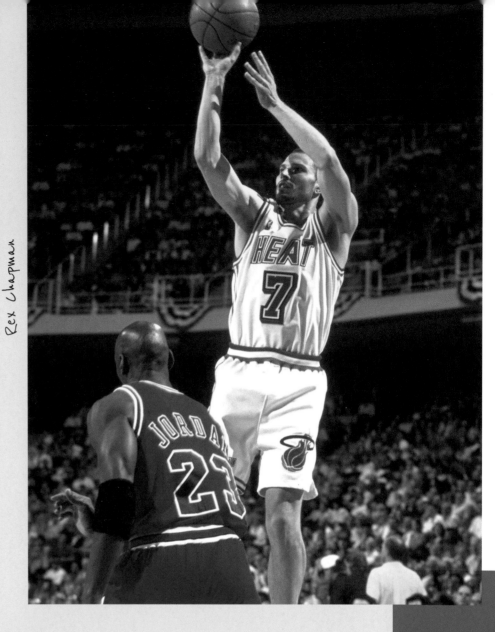

Rex Chapman

CRAZY EIGHTS

CHICAGO VS. MIAMI, FEBRUARY 23, 1996

The Heat had just made a blockbuster trade. Three-time All-Star Tim
Hardaway and four other players were on their way to Miami. But they
wouldn't arrive in time for the game that night. "It was a throwaway game to
me," said Heat coach Pat Riley. "We had eight guys. We had to hustle guard
Tony Smith in here quick just to be legal." Shooting guard Rex Chapman lived
up to his team's nickname. He was on fire, sinking 9 of 10 three-point shots
and finishing with 39 points. "Rex just had one of those nights," Riley said.
Miami won 113–104. It was one of only 10 Bulls losses that season.

Tim Hardaway

Conference. Riley was named NBA Coach of the Year. This time there would be no early playoff exit. Miami won the first two rounds. They faced Chicago in the Eastern Conference finals. Once again, the Bulls had too much firepower. Miami won just one game in the series.

The Heat won the Atlantic Division in each of the next three seasons. They also had a new nemesis: the New York Knicks. The Heat had defeated the Knicks in the 1997 playoffs. The Knicks returned the favor in 1998. The same thing happened the following season. That series was especially disheartening. Miami was the top seed. They lost the deciding Game 5 by a single point on a jump shot with less than a second remaining on the clock. "Life in basketball has a lot of suffering in it," Riley said. "And we will suffer this one."

The suffering at the hands of the Knicks continued the following season. This time the teams met in the second round. Again, the Heat lost by a single point in the final game. The four-year rivalry was intense. It was packed with fights and close games. "From a competitive standpoint … it was some of the best basketball that's ever been played," Riley said.

THE HEAT GETTING HOTTER

The 2000–01 season began with bad news. Mourning had a rare kidney disease. He missed most of the season. His teammates wanted to pick up the slack. "This is an opportunity for the rest of us to lead in his absence," said shooting guard/small forward Dan Majerle. "We won't quit, because we owe that to Zo." Miami went on to win 50 games. But the Charlotte Hornets swept the Heat in the first round of the playoffs. They slumped to 36 wins the following season. It was the first time in Riley's 20-year head coaching career that his team didn't make the playoffs. The Heat did even worse in 2002–03. Mourning had to sit out the entire season to take care of his health. He became a free agent and signed with the New Jersey Nets. Without him, the Heat won only 25 games.

Miami drafted Dwyane Wade with the fifth overall selection of the 2003 NBA Draft. He sparked the Heat to 42 wins and the second round of the playoffs. Miami made a monster trade for massive center Shaquille O'Neal after the season. "Today, the Miami Heat took a giant step forward in our continued pursuit of an NBA championship for the city of Miami and this franchise," Riley said.

The trade paid off. With Shaq dominating the middle, Miami surged to a 59–23 mark. The Heat swept their opponents in the first two rounds of the playoffs. Then they faced the Detroit Pistons in the Eastern Conference finals. Miami took a 3–2 series edge. But Wade suffered a painful rib injury in Game 5. He missed Game 6. The Pistons dominated the Heat, 91–66. "Obviously, not having him [Wade], that impacted the game so much," said Pistons coach Larry Brown. Wade returned for Game 7 but played hurt. "He didn't have his explosiveness," said Miami point/shooting guard Keyon Dooling. "He was in a lot of pain." Detroit took the series with an 88–82 win.

Dwyane Wade

LEGENDS
OF THE HARDWOOD

NEW YORK VS. MIAMI
EASTERN CONFERENCE SEMIFINALS
GAME 5
MAY 14, 1997

CHAOS ON THE COURT

With less than two minutes left, Heat power forward P. J. Brown grabbed Knicks point guard Charlie Ward under the basket and hurled him head over heels into the first row of spectators. Several Knicks rushed into the melee. Five— including their top two scorers—were suspended for Game 6. Brown was suspended for two games. The players were also fined. Those penalties were the league's most severe for fighting during the playoffs. Miami won the game, 96–81. That prevented the Knicks from closing out the series. Miami went on to win the next two games and take the series.

TAKING THE TITLE

The Heat won 52 games in 2005–06. Again, they faced Detroit in the Eastern Conference finals. Miami won the series, 4 games to 2. Now they took on the Dallas Mavericks for the NBA title. They lost the first two games. A loss in Game 3 would effectively end their season. No team had ever come back from a 3–0 deficit in a best-of-seven series. With the score tied in the final seconds, 16-year veteran shooting guard Gary Payton's 18-foot jumper gave them the win. Wade had 42 points. He kept his foot on the gas in the next three games. He scored 36 points, then 43, then 36 again. Miami won all three games to win the NBA championship, 4 games to 2. They were only the third team in NBA history to win the title after losing the first two games of the series. Wade was an obvious choice for Finals Most Valuable Player (MVP). "I didn't have the best game," said O'Neal. "But D-Wade's been doing it all year. He's the best player ever."

Heat fans hoped for a repeat title the following season. Wade suffered a severe shoulder injury and missed nearly half the season. Miami did win 44 games, but Chicago swept them in the first round of the playoffs. Wade missed nearly half of the 2007–08 season with a knee injury. O'Neal was traded mid-season. Miami won just 15 games. That matched the franchise's worst record. Wade was fully healthy the following season. He led the league in scoring with an average of 30.2 points per game. The Heat's two draft choices, forward Michael Beasley and point guard Mario Chalmers, made important contributions. Miami improved to 43–39. They lost to Atlanta in the first round of the playoffs. The Heat won 47 games the following season. Again, they made an early playoff exit, falling to the Boston Celtics, 4 games to 1.

Wade became a free agent after the 2009–10 season. Miami wanted him to stay. Local officials renamed Miami-Dade County as Miami-Wade County for a week. On the other hand, Wade had grown up in Chicago. The Bulls wanted him to come home and play for them. It was a tough decision. Wade asked family members to vote. It was a tie. The "tiebreaker" was Chris Bosh, who was also a free agent. He announced that he was moving south from Toronto to play for Miami. Wade immediately said he would stay. There was another prize free agent: LeBron James. He had become a superstar with the Cleveland Cavaliers. Less than 48 hours after Bosh's announcement, James signed with Miami. The three players quickly became nicknamed the "Big Three." "You have three guys, All-Stars, in the prime of their career," said Orlando Magic coach Stan Van Gundy. "That's a heckuva team to match up against."

THE "BIG THREE" ERA

Dwyane Wade, Chris Bosh, and LeBron James became known as the "Big Three." Teams often had trouble matching up with the "Big Three" and their teammates. The Heat won 58 games during the 2010–11 season. But the Mavericks defeated Miami in the NBA Finals, 4 games to 2. The Heat added Ray Allen before the lockout-shortened 2011–12 season. They dominated the Oklahoma City Thunder in the NBA Finals, 4 games to 1. "Winning

LeBron James

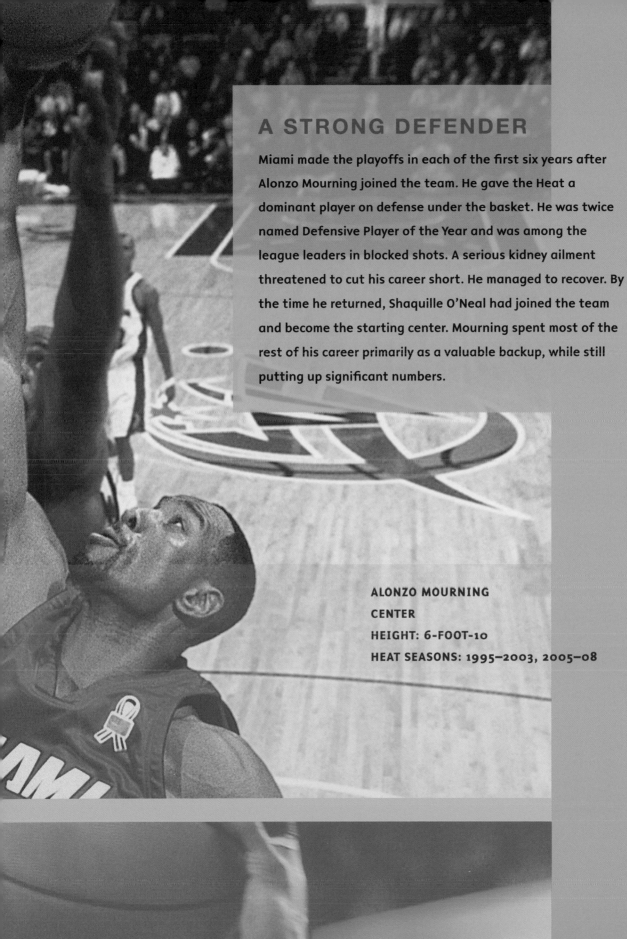

A STRONG DEFENDER

Miami made the playoffs in each of the first six years after Alonzo Mourning joined the team. He gave the Heat a dominant player on defense under the basket. He was twice named Defensive Player of the Year and was among the league leaders in blocked shots. A serious kidney ailment threatened to cut his career short. He managed to recover. By the time he returned, Shaquille O'Neal had joined the team and become the starting center. Mourning spent most of the rest of his career primarily as a valuable backup, while still putting up significant numbers.

ALONZO MOURNING
CENTER
HEIGHT: 6-FOOT-10
HEAT SEASONS: 1995–2003, 2005–08

a championship, it's the reason that we all came here together," Wade said. "And I'm not just talking about Chris, LeBron, and myself…. I'm talking about all these guys." The year was especially memorable for James. He joined Michael Jordan as the only players to win the NBA championship, MVP award, Finals MVP award, and Olympic gold medal in the same year.

Miami had its best year ever in 2012–13, winning 66 games. That included a 27-game winning streak. It was the second-longest single-season streak in NBA history! They romped through the first two rounds of the playoffs. After edging the Indiana Pacers, 4 games to 3, in the Eastern Conference finals, the Heat defeated the Spurs to win their second straight title.

Miami fans felt confident that the team would win its third straight championship the following season. Again, they faced the Spurs with the title at stake. With the series tied at a game apiece, the Spurs won the next three games by an average of 19 points. James left Miami soon afterward. He returned to Cleveland. The Heat added two-time All-Star small forward Luol Deng and center Hassan Whiteside to try to make up for losing James. But Bosh missed nearly half the season due to injuries and health issues. The Heat stumbled to a 37–45 mark.

They rebounded in 2015–16 to win 48 games. Miami lost to the Toronto Raptors in the second round of the playoffs. In a stunning move, Wade left the Heat to return to his hometown of Chicago and play for the Bulls.

Miami made just one playoff appearance in the next three seasons, losing in the first round to the 76ers in 2017–18. It was a different story in the COVID-19-shortened 2019–20 season. To the surprise of many people, the Heat romped

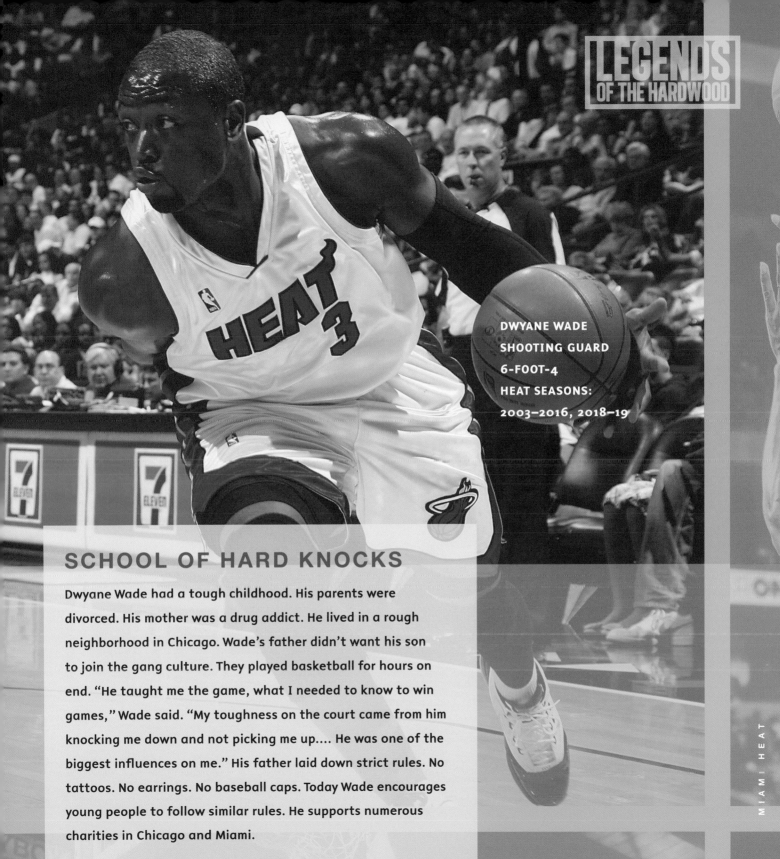

DWYANE WADE
SHOOTING GUARD
6-FOOT-4
HEAT SEASONS:
2003–2016, 2018–19

SCHOOL OF HARD KNOCKS

Dwyane Wade had a tough childhood. His parents were divorced. His mother was a drug addict. He lived in a rough neighborhood in Chicago. Wade's father didn't want his son to join the gang culture. They played basketball for hours on end. "He taught me the game, what I needed to know to win games," Wade said. "My toughness on the court came from him knocking me down and not picking me up.... He was one of the biggest influences on me." His father laid down strict rules. No tattoos. No earrings. No baseball caps. Today Wade encourages young people to follow similar rules. He supports numerous charities in Chicago and Miami.

MIAMI HEAT

Jimmy Butler

through the first three rounds of the playoffs. Veteran swingman Jimmy Butler averaged 20 points a game in his first season in South Florida, power forward Bam Adebayo became an All-Star, and rookie shooting guard Tyler Herro showed great promise for the future. The Heat faced the Lakers and James in the Finals. The former Miami star was named series MVP as he led Los Angeles to a 4–2 win.

Milwaukee swept Miami in the first round of the playoffs in the following season. In 2021–22, Miami was consistently among the leaders in the Eastern Conference. A six-game winning streak at the end of the season gave them a 53–29 record and the top seed in the conference playoffs. Herro averaged nearly 21 points a game off the bench. He became the first Miami player to be named the NBA Sixth Man of the Year.

Miami defeated Atlanta, 4 games to 1, in the first round of the playoffs. They beat Philadelphia, 4 games to 2, in the conference semifinals. The Heat faced Boston in the Eastern Conference finals. Butler raised his game to another level against the Celtics. "Jimmy is a great competitor," said coach Eric Spoelstra. "I think he's one of the ultimate competitors in the game." Butler averaged more than 27 points a game, including a playoff career-high 47 in the Game 6 victory that extended the series to the full seven games. But Boston won Game 7, 100–96, to take the series.

Since their founding more than 30 years ago, the Miami Heat have become a popular sports franchise in South Florida. Three titles over an eight-season stretch in the 21st century have given fans a thirst for more. They hope to see another championship banner in the near future.

Max Strus

INDEX